Yosemite Nat  k

Scavenger Hunt and Bucket List

Moonstone Mountaineer

Table of Contents

Remember to NEVER approach or feed wildlife!

Black Bear

Black bears can come in many colors including auburn, honey, brown, and black. Look in the meadows especially around dusk or dawn if trying to spot one of these iconic animals.

80 points

Western Tanager

These strikingly beautiful birds can be found flitting about the campgrounds, enjoying a cool drink from the Merced River, or singing in the pines.

65 points

Mule Deer

Typically found in meadows and open areas, mule deer, believe it or not, are the most dangerous animals in Yosemite. There are more injuries due to mule deer than any other animal in the park. They may look unassuming but they are capable of doing some damage should you get too close!

30 points

Remember to NEVER approach or feed wildlife!

Ground Squirrel

From running around picnic tables to scampering across sidewalks, you're sure to spot at least one of these little guys on your adventures!

10 points

Steller's Jay

See that flash of blue streaking through the trees? That a Steller's Jay! Their unique call is like an ode to Yosemite.

25 points

Coyote

Look to the meadows or even the side of the road for these coyotes. Slow down while driving to help protect these beautiful animals and all wildlife of Yosemite National Park.

45 points

Remember to NEVER approach or feed wildlife!

Bobcat

These elusive creatures are hard to spot, hence the high reward if you see one.
Agile and stealthy, consider yourself lucky should you spot one of these spotted cats.

90 points

Fisher Cat

Usually seen at night , these little guys can scare you by popping out from behind trees.
A rare sight.

85 points

Mountain Lion

Hopefully you **don't** see one of these!
Remember, if you ever encounter a mountain lion, stay calm - never turn your back and run!
Back away slowly while still facing the lion, shout, and make yourself large.
If attacked, fight back!

100 points

Remember to NEVER approach or feed wildlife!

Sierra Nevada Red Fox

Typically seen in meadows, these red foxes are smaller than most foxes around the world. Their fur is also darker than most foxes and they retain a spot on the endangered species list.

95 points

Great Gray Owl

Perhaps you'll see their shadow fly above your campfire or hear their hoots in the early morning. These great owls are nearly impossible to spot due to their nocturnal habits and how rare they are.

100 points

Bighorn Sheep

Look to the rocky slopes of the high country and maybe you'll see one of these extremely shy sheep. Both male and female sheep have horns, however, the male's horns are typically bigger.

100 points

Remember to NEVER approach or feed wildlife!

Peregrine Falcon

Get your binoculars out and look up to the granite cliffsides! These protected birds of prey are known for their precariously placed nests that live thousands of feet above the valley floor.

90 points

Gartersnake

Should one of these snakes cross your path, do not fear as they are not venomous and only want to slither by.

65 points

Pileated Woodpecker

This woodpecker is unique in that it has a rather large point on the back of its head that makes the creature look almost dinosaur-like. The striking red is easy to spot, as well as the tell-tale sound of pecking.

75 points

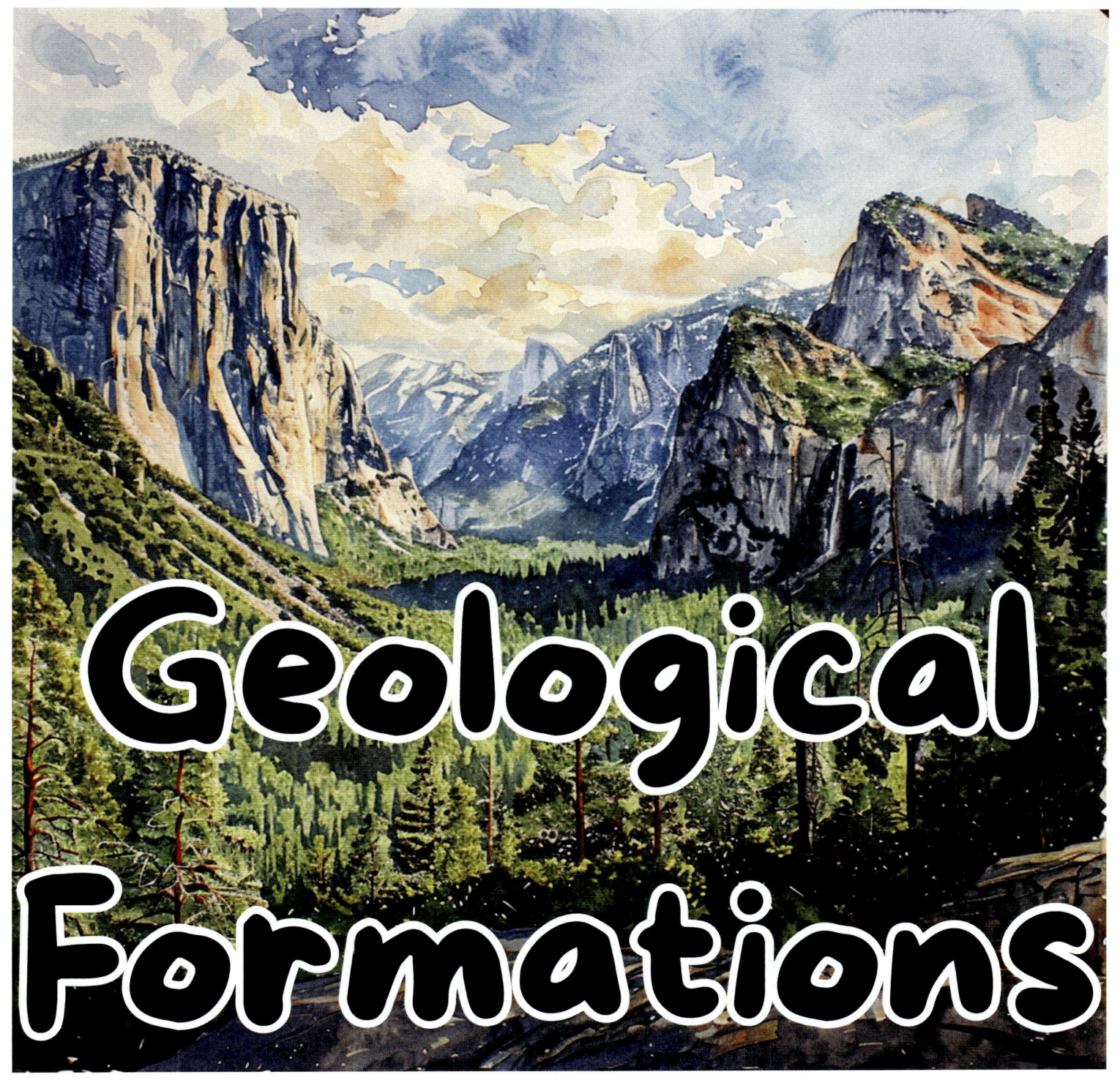

Glacial ice made this place real nice!

Half Dome

This iconic granite rock face is a rite of passage for rock climbers as well as a daring adventure for brave hikers. Grab some binoculars. Can you see anyone climbing? Or perhaps, if you are looking from Olmsted Point, you can spy the cables where hikers brave the steep dome.

25 points

Upper Yosemite Falls

The tallest waterfall in North America, Yosemite Falls is a sight to see! Often times in spring, the sound of this roaring waterfall can be heard echoing across the valley floor.

25 points

Lower Yosemite Falls

Take the one mile round trip hike to see the rush that is Lower Yosemite Falls! John Muir used to live just below this incredible water feature.

30 points

Glacial ice made this place real nice!

El Capitan

This aptly named monolith is a testament to the true Yosemite spirit! Climbers from around the world come to try their hand at defeating this granite wall which stretches higher than the Empire State Building. At night, the lights from these climbers closely resemble that of stars glittering in the sky.

25 points

Bridalveil Fall

The legend goes: Those kissed by the mist will be married within one year's time! Whether this myth is true or not remains to be seen, however there's no mistaking the wonder that ensues when gazing upon this epic waterfall!

25 points

Fern Spring

This lesser known feature is a cool spot to stop and see a natural spring that used to have fresh drinking water readily available. Now the water is unpotable due to contamination but the spring itself is still beautiful to see.

45 points

Glacial ice made this place real nice!

Vernal Fall

Hike the iconic Mist Trail to see this rainbow infused waterfall! If hiking in the early spring, be prepared to get soaked as, like the trail name implies, you're gonna get wet!

45 points

Nevada Fall

Further up the Mist Trail is this incredible waterfall that looks almost slide-like. Don't be tempted however as these waters are dangerous and swift!

55 points

Lembert Dome

Adventure to the high country where you can find this angular dome displayed in all of its glory in Tuolomne Meadows.

65 points

Glacial ice made this place real nice!

Soda Springs

This unique spring brings forth quite the vibrant colors as well as clean drinking water for the animals nearby.

65 points

The Three Brothers

These epic granite points jut out from the earth in a dramatic array of splendor! Perhaps you'll be lucky enough to spot these hidden gems whilst on a drive around the valley!

45 points

Sentinel Rock

Just like a sentinel, this rock stands watch over the valley, and more specifically, Cook's Meadow. Towering thousands of feet above the valley floor, this iconic landmark is a reminder of how strong Yosemite is.

35 points

Plants and Trees

Leave those wildflowers be so others may see!

Ponderosa Pine

Scratch and sniff! No really. Scratch at the bark of a ponderosa pine and you'll be craving sweets. This bark smells uniquely like sugar!

20 points

Redbud

These beautiful flowering bushes can only be seen March through May. Their flowers, which range from pink to red, line Highway 140 like a red carpet leading you to Yosemite.

55 points

Manzanita

These bushy plants are easily recognizable by their red limbs and smooth bark.

45 points

Leave those wildflowers be so others may see!

Giant Sequoia

These larger than life trees are some of the largest in the world! Go to Mariposa Grove or Tuolumne Grove to enjoy their awe-inspiring size.

45 points

Lupine

There's nothing like the feeling of driving through Yosemite on a summer's day, breathing in the mountain air, and viewing the gorgeous Lupine that decorates the roadsides.

35 points

Dogwood

When the white flowers bloom, you forget all of your gloom! An extra **25 bonus points** on top of the points below if you find one of the ultra-rare pink Dogwoods in Yosemite Valley.

65 points

Leave those wildflowers be so others may see!

Snow Plant

Despite the name, this unique plant can be found flowering late May and June. It is when the snow melts that this bright flowers emerges.

95 points

California Poppy

California's State flower can be seen dotting the hills of Yosemite creating waves of popping orange color.

45 points

Black Oak Tree

Scattered around Yosemite, the Black Oak is an important symbol of Yosemite's strength and resilience. The bark for these unique oaks are dark, almost black.

35 points

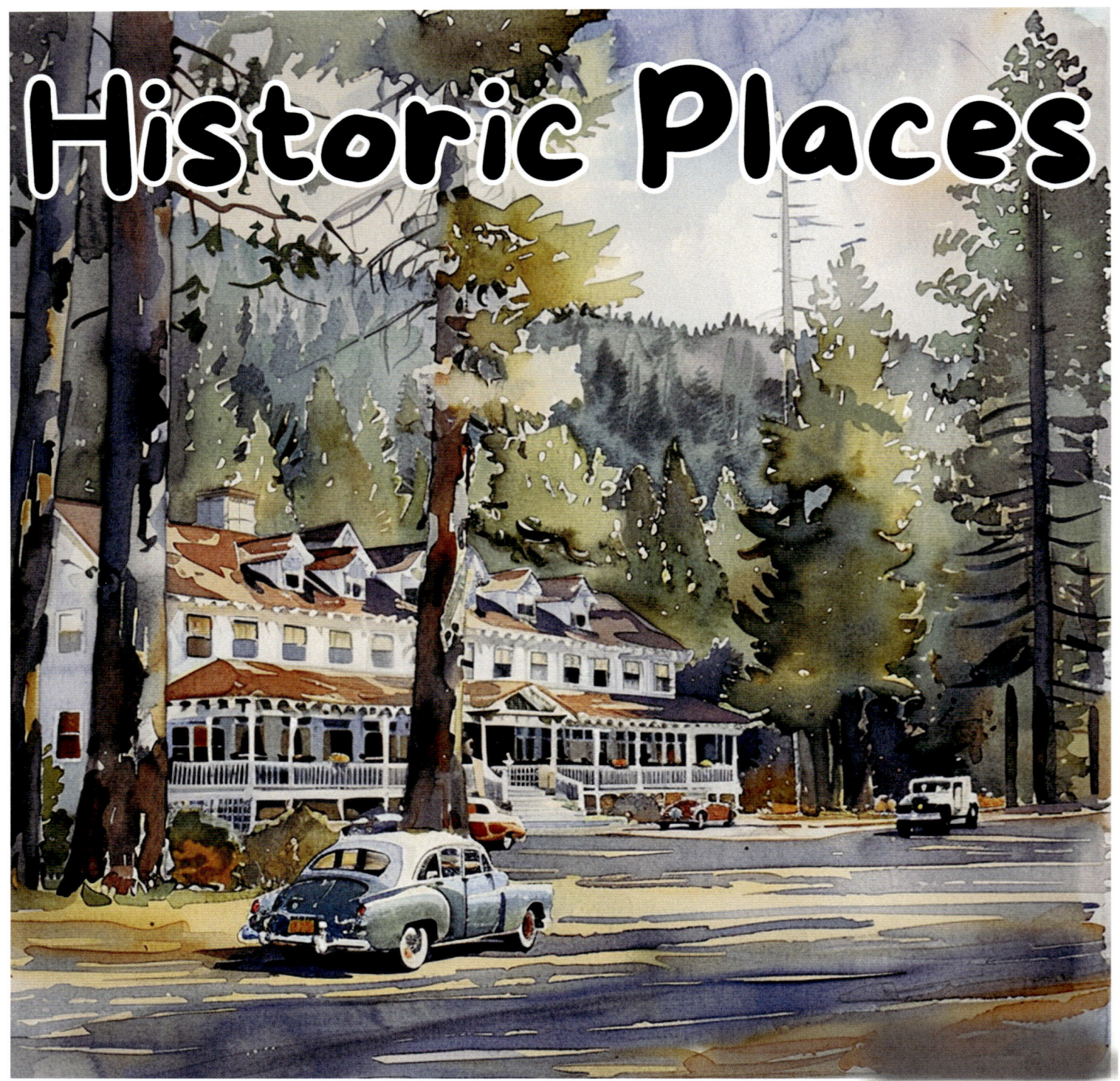

Historic Places

John Muir would be happy to see you here!

Midnight Lightning

Gather round and watch as boulderers from around the world attempt this difficult ascent. Located in the back of Camp 4, this difficult boulder has an iconic chalk lightening bolt marking its existence.

55 points

The Ahwanhee Hotel

This historic hotel is known for its views and spectacular architecture. This is a great place to cozy up with a book, especially on a winter day.

35 points

The Yosemite Cemetery

This cemetery, built in the 1870's, is the final resting place of several notable figures in Yosemite's history. Take a quiet walk around and see who you find.

35 points

John Muir would be happy to see you here!

The Wawona Hotel

This hotel is hard to miss if you're entering the park through the South Entrance on Highway 140. The hotel was created in 1876 to house tourists visiting the Mariposa Grove of Giant Sequoias.

35 points

Yosemite History Center

Right next to the Wawona Hotel is the Yosemite History Center, or in other words, a step into the past. See historic buildings, horse-drawn carriages, and Chris Jorgensen's artist cabin.

45 points

The Yosemite Museum

Looking to learn more about Yosemite's history? This is a wonderful place to see artifacts and learn about the seven indigenous tribes that call this place home.

65 points

John Muir would be happy to see you here!

Muir and Roosevelt

Visit the marker where John Muir and Theodore Roosevelt camped. This is where they talked in depth about conservation efforts and Muir helped Roosevelt make decisions that would change the future of Yosemite forever.

25 points

John Muir's Cabin

There's no cabin to see here but there is a plaque on a rock. The adventurous spirit of John Muir can be imagined listening to the roar of Yosemite Falls and knowing this is where he called home.

35 points

Swinging Bridge

What once was actually a swinging bridge, hence the name, had to be replaced after the flood of 1997. Enjoy an incredible view of Yosemite Falls from this bridge.

35 points

John Muir would be happy to see you here!

Happy Isles Nature Center

More focused on natural history, this is a great place for kids to learn about the park's wildlife or experience some interactive art workshops.

65 points

Curry Village

Originally Camp Curry, this village of tent cabins has been known for it's location and amenities since 1899. While no longer run by The Curry Company, the village still exists and thrives to this day.

25 points

The Yosemite Valley Lodge

Located close enough to hear Yosemite Falls, this hotel is a great place to pick up the popular Valley Floor Tour, otherwise known as the green dragon.

25 points

Viewpoints

Enjoy the view, I know you'll do!

Glacier Point

Glacier Point is known for it's brilliant view of Half Dome as well as the valley as a whole. Towering above Curry Village, you can see all the way from Yosemite Falls to Nevada Falls and beyond.

45 points

Washburn Point

This view, not far from Glacier point, shows another angle of Half Dome and surrounding mountains.

55 points

Taft Point

This point will take a short hike but the view is worth it! Another striking visage of Yosemite Valley.

65 points

Enjoy the view, I know you'll do!

Olmsted Point

Catch a glimpse of the iconic Half Dome from the other side! A sight not so often depicted, this rare side of Half Dome can be seen from Tioga Pass when the seasonal road is open.

25 points

Tunnel View

Get ready to have your breath taken away! Right when you exit the tunnel on Highway 41 (hence the name) you'll see sweeping views of the valley all the way from Bridalveil and El Capitan to Half Dome!

35 points

Valley View

Down on the valley floor, get a grand view of El Capitan and Bridal Veil all whilst soaking in the rush of standing next to the Merced River.

35 points

Don't forget these fun things!

Firefall

Only visible for a limited time every year, Firefall is a photographer's dream adventure! Every year in February people from around the world come to witness this phenomenon where Horsetail Fall glows bright orange in the sunlight, much like fire.

85 points

Ansel Adam's Gallery

Visit this gallery which features not only the iconic photography of Ansel Adam's but also a plethora of other art from various artists!

25 points

Hike Half Dome

Make sure you have a permit and understand the risks before taking this daring hike!

95 points

Don't forget these fun things!

Stargazing

Half the Park is after dark! Or so the saying goes. Don't miss out on Yosemite's spectacular star display, whether you go to Glacier Point for viewing or stay down in the valley.

45 points

Ephemeral Waterfalls

There are many waterfalls in Yosemite with no names, especially in spring. These unnamed waterfalls are called ephemeral waterfalls. Add **10 points** for every extra one you spot!

25 points

Spotting Climbers

Look to the skies! Or to the granite cliff faces rather. Look with binoculars or just your eyes to try and spot one of these brave climbers around Yosemite!

65 points

Super Extra Mega Awesome Extreme Bonus!

100 points

While this isn't the most unachievable destination, I've given this task a high score because of its personal meaning to me. I want you to visit my very favorite place in Yosemite! I have a lot of special spots in mind but this one takes the cake. It's simple really. All you have to do is take the short walk on the bike path in between the Yosemite Valley Lodge and Swinging Bridge. Along the way you'll find my favorite spot in the whole park! The view of Cathedral Rocks beyond the meadow leaves me breathless every time I see it. Something about the way the light hits those granite monoliths just right, especially on a summer evening, sets my heart aflame and reminds me of the true spirit and energy of Yosemite. I hope you all can experience this at least one time during your visit. And when you walk down that path and see what I see, I hope you think of me at least once! I really enjoyed creating this book and hope you all have a wonderful adventure in Yosemite!

Made in United States
Orlando, FL
25 May 2025

61572439R00019